Like. Follow. Lead.

Mastering Social Media for Small Business

By Nerissa Golden

Cover design by Karibgraphics, Trinidad & Tobago

Logos used remain the property of the respective companies and brands.

ISBN-13: 978-1500139902

DEDICATION

To the entrepreneurs who get tempted but never give up.

CONTENTS

ACKNOWLEDGMENTS

Carol Ottley-Mitchell you always ask me the right questions at the time I most need to have an answer.

Forever grateful that you know how to put pictures to my words Kathryn Duncan.

Ursula Barzey of Moxee Marketing – the Social Media guru.

Linda Linda Linda. You always back my crazy ideas. Thank you.

Nia Golden, I'm really glad you are on my team. Thank you for believing in me.

1

A Crash Course in Social Media

Is your business taking full advantage of social media and the potential it has for turning your local venture into a global one?

While many of us are comfortable using Skype, FaceTime, and even Google Hangouts to keep Grandma up to date with Little Johnny's latest antics, we struggle when it comes to using these tools to improve how we communicate for business.

And with good reason. With over 3000 social media platforms it is a daunting task to figure out what social space is the right one for your business and how to use them in order to get results.

The ideas presented here will give you a starting point for understanding how to use social media to push your business to the front of the line in your sector. Using the tools below, you will increase exposure for your business and attract clients who want your services and products.

For the purposes of this book, we will only reference the most popular social media platforms and present simple ways in which you can use them to engage with your clients.

First, let's review some of the more popular social media networks and/or platforms today.

POPULAR SOCIAL MEDIA SPACES

(In alphabetical order)

Blogs

Many people think of their blog as a website but while they can be connected, these two marketing tools have distinct purposes. Your website shares static information about you and your company, for example, the year it was founded, the services you offer, the key team members, and where your office is located.

Your blog can and should be a section of your site which gives current information about what your company is doing. This may include events you've hosted, news releases, and most importantly current articles with tips and other details that let your customers know that you are an expert in your field.

Make it easier for people to comment and share your articles and content by including social share options such as sharethis.com or addthis.com.

Facebook

This social networking site has transformed the way the world does business. It is now an expectation that a company, no matter the size, has a Facebook Fan Page to be considered legitimate and "with it". Individuals must "like" your page in order to see the information you share. The built-in measurement system provides data on which of your posts are generating the most interaction.

Another option is to start a Group, which should be focused on people with similar interests or private for clients in a special program you are offering.

Women and young adults 18 to 29 are the top users of this site, which has over 1.15 billion monthly active users.

Google Plus

Part of the growing Google Family, this networking space with 359 million monthly active users is quickly gaining traction as a legitimate space to promote and do business. By integrating Google Plus with other products such as Gmail, Google Hangout, YouTube, and Google Drive, you can have a virtual office complete with networking and communication tools.

According to socialstatistics.com, Google Plus is heavily favored by males, with the majority being fairly well educated with a background in technology based fields like web development and software engineering.

Instagram

More than 150 million users enjoy this platform, which allows you to share beautiful images altered with filters to express your unique view of the world and your personality. While still growing in popularity, this platform works excellently for travel bloggers, food critics, destinations and brands that understand customer engagement. Instagram supports the use of hashtags (discussed in depth later in the book) to allow you to promote your images and to reach an audience beyond your Instagram followers.

LinkedIn

Now the third most popular social media platform with 250 million users, LinkedIn is a more formal platform for business. Where you might show a bit of a lighter side of your business image on Facebook with a photo of your family or your pet, these are not the images for LinkedIn. LinkedIn enables you to expand your network to include people you may not know personally but who can add value to your associations and become team members on future projects. LinkedIn users typically range between 25 to 64 years of age.

Pinterest

Who would have thought a virtual pinboard would be good for business? It is. Companies use it primarily to showcase products on offer and to build brand recognition. Users can search the vast catalogue of photos by interest area, then "like" and pin images that they would like to purchase, recipes to try at a later date, or a suggested quick fix for a household chore. This platform differs from Facebook as Pinterest is more about showcasing your interests and less about creating relationships and discussions around a product. Women are the primary users of Pinterest, which has just over 20 million monthly active users.

Skype

While not considered a social media platform in the traditional sense, it is included as an important element of marketing and communications for small and large businesses. This service began as a place to make free voice calls over the internet, however, with its group call option it gives businesses an extra benefit for doing interviews, collaborating with consultants abroad, and meeting with clients. There are many business applications for Skype, for example, a new option to have video group chats makes it another go-to platform for conducting a webinar or training for staff and customers.

Twitter

Tell a story in 140 characters or less. This is the challenge for the 215 million monthly Twitter users and one that they take on every day for a myriad of reasons. More than 27 million tweets are sent daily on this platform and while it can seem an intimidating space, it is possible to gain traction for your cause or business on Twitter. The majority of users are women and young adults between the ages of 18 and 29. African-Americans make up a large portion of its users.

YouTube

This is the second most searched site behind its parent company Google's search engine. More than 1 billion people use YouTube every month and over 6 billion hours of video are watched. Companies should consider using this medium to share promotional videos about what they do. Entrepreneurs can create videos that share their story and encourage viewers to engage with them offline. Using relevant tags will enable your videos to be found much easier by potential customers.

2

How Can Social Media Help Your Business?

Whether your business is a small town operation or an online company, which serves clients globally, you can benefit from having an active social media presence.

Social Media ought to be a part of your company's overall strategy to grow your business and increase your brand's exposure.

Your social spaces should be about doing things that will increase your company's visibility, attract new customers and make you money. Your goals for social media need to go deeper than "we want to gain 500 fans on Facebook or 200 Twitter followers."

Be very clear about what you want to accomplish online.

❖ Increase brand awareness.
❖ Attract new customers.
❖ Launch a new product.
❖ Get feedback on our present services.

Understanding what you want to achieve will help you in designing your campaigns and interactions and selecting the most appropriate platforms.

Here's an example:

Fine Apparel, Nevis, W.I.

Karen Beaumont is a seamstress in Nevis who works from her home. She wants to gain new clients for her business. She's heard that Facebook is a good way to get more customers but has no idea what to do and where to start.

Is Facebook the right place for Karen? Before setting up her business on any social platform, Karen needs to ask herself a few questions including the following:

- ❖ Who is her ideal customer?
- ❖ How many new customers can she serve and in what period of time?
- ❖ What investment would she need to make to deliver the best quality clothing, in a reasonable time?
- ❖ Which social platforms are her ideal customers on?
- ❖ How much time can she invest in managing her social media?
- ❖ What can she offer potential customers who connect with her online?
- ❖ How can she serve clients overseas who may want her to make outfits for them?

Answering these questions will guide Karen in planning for growth and how she uses her social media platforms.

Once you know what your goals are, set your targets for your online campaign but make sure they are **SMART**.

Specific

Measurable

Achievable

Realistic

Time Bound.

Examples of SMART Goals

- "Get 10 fans who are resident on Nevis to visit Fine Apparel within two weeks."
- "Increase orders for school uniforms by 20% following this one-month campaign."
- "Encourage 10 young professionals to register for our summer design challenge."

Which Social Media Platform Fits Your Business?

With goals and targets in hand, it's time to pick the vehicle for achieving them. There is no "one size fits all". Just as you engage with your friends in different ways, so you must know where your customers are and how to connect with them.

Facebook and Twitter are considered the social media powerhouse brands. You need to approach each of them differently. What works for Facebook is not ideal for Twitter.

Twitter is time intensive as it is important to keep conversations going in real time and that may not be possible if you are your business' only employee.

If your company is primarily product-driven and you need large numbers of people to see what you offer, then Pinterest and Facebook could be your social media match. These sites allow for posting photos of your products, events, or services with supporting details. Pinterest, however gives you more real estate to post larger images so potential customers will see more detail than they would on Facebook. Your images can be hyperlinked directly to your website where pinners can be encouraged to buy your product or gain more information.

For authors and speakers, spaces such as Twitter and YouTube might be a more appropriate fit as you can share witty or profound quotes from your books or the books of other authors you like and post videos around the subject matter that is important to you, all of which can lead to sales or speaking opportunities. Authors should also make use of GoodReads, Amazon.com's author pages, and Facebook groups and pages that cater to your audience niche.

Consultants can do well on LinkedIn where your goal is to make connections to find potential clients, collaborate with other professionals or to find a new job. However, if it's not a primary space for your target market then it is best not to establish a LinkedIn presence if your time is limited. A blog can also help to generate interest in your consulting business. Consider sharing white papers, presentations, and free downloads on your blog or via platforms such as SlideShare. Using Google Hangouts and/or Skype to hold small webinars are other ways you can drum up exposure for your business.

Photographers who serve clients in the corporate arena should consider LinkedIn as it now provides opportunity for showcasing a portfolio of your work.

Instagram is great for luxury goods, artists, chefs, resorts, and creative thinkers who capture the world in unique ways. Authors, professional speakers, and actors can create brand exposure here as well. The downside to this platform is that you can only have a clickable web link in your profile and not on the image or in the comments. This means your image needs to be compelling to encourage followers to take the extra step and search for the link or to find more information about you.

Chefs can use YouTube to showcase their cooking skills and teach 'how-to' cooking workshops. The platform also allows for live cooking demonstrations. Teachers, entertainers, web developers can also find success here. YouTube is about sharing content and no matter your area of interest it is a place that allows you add to the online conversations and provide information for potential customers to access.

Suggested Social Media for Your Specific Business

Here is a summary of the information presented in this chapter.

Business	YouTube	f	Instagram	Pinterest	Twitter	g+	in	Skype
Advertising/Marketing		☺		☺	☺	☺		☺
Accounting/Law		☺					☺	☺
Author/Speaking/Training	☺	☺			☺	☺	☺	☺
Food & Beverage	☺	☺	☺	☺			☺	☺
Health Care		☺				☺	☺	☺
Fashion & Beauty	☺	☺	☺	☺				☺
Filmmaking/Music	☺	☺	☺			☺		☺
Graphics Design		☺	☺			☺	☺	☺
Photography		☺	☺	☺			☺	☺
Hotel/B&B	☺	☺	☺	☺	☺	☺		☺
Web Development		☺			☺	☺	☺	☺
News Media /Television	☺	☺			☺	☺		☺
Politics/Government	☺	☺			☺	☺	☺	☺

3

Like

Facebook with more than one billion active users is the primary social media platform at the time of this publication. Developed in 2004, it has become a space where the business and the personal can collide or co-exist if you understand how to use it.

Although Facebook is free to join, the company has increasingly pushed the use of paid promotions, especially since it became a publicly traded company in 2012. In this way, they encourage you to purchase additional exposure for your products or services.

Facebook employs the Like concept, which was created as a way for friends to quickly give you a thumb's up without need for words. Users can 'like' your page. Once they do this, they will receive updates about what your company is offering.

Let's discuss some of the features of Facebook in more detail.

Fan Page Vs Profile

I have many friends who joined Facebook for the sole purpose of promoting a business but they created a Profile which is designed to focus on a person and not on a company. While some have found success using their profile to hawk their wares, they are missing out on important marketing information that can be gathered when using a Fan Page.

While both the Profile and the Fan Page allow you to share photos, contact information, and other details about your company, the Profile does not give you the option to analyze the demographics of your customers. Unless you know all 5000 of your Profile contacts personally, you need a way of understanding where they are, who they are and how they interact with the content you share and your products. You can then use this knowledge to better target your marketing and your product offering. For example:

> Jane is selling her winter boots online. She has 750 fans, but they are all from the Caribbean. She needs to redirect her effort to gain more exposure in colder climates; however, since she is unaware of the nature of her contacts, she has no idea why Facebook is not working for her as a marketing mechanism.

A Fan Page gives you this data. Once you've acquired more than 30 Likes or Fans, Facebook allows you to see insights of who is visiting your page and where they are. You can learn whether photos, inspirational tips or how-to articles attract the most attention, whether your visitors are male or female and other details which can help you tweak your content and increase engagement and the positive impact of your business.

Jane should consider purchasing Facebook ads targeted at the colder countries to increase exposure of her boots. She should also consider connecting with fashion brands in the countries she's most keen to sell to and develop a relationship which can lead to joint promotions.

What Times Are Best To Share?

Quite a bit of research has been done about the best time of the day to share information on Facebook and other social media to increase interaction from your fans. Some results suggest early in the morning between 6am and 8am when people are just waking up or getting to the office and also after 7pm when others are at home and are relaxing for the night. Weekends are also said to be good times to post.

How do you know what will work for your fans and their connections? Test them all.

Start with you. What is your social media pattern of usage? Are you a night owl and most likely to be on after 10pm? Do you check your phone the minute your eyes open in the morning? Are you one of those people that work with your Facebook open and respond to every notification sound?

Take a note of your social media pattern and that of your friends for two weeks. How often do you interact with the Fan Pages you like? What do they share that gets you the most inspired and motivated to click Like, Share or Comment? Is this similar to what your friends do on your timeline?

Regularly review your Facebook notifications and activity register to see what time of day and how frequently fans engage with your page. Did you share a photo that got everyone talking or sharing? Were they inspired by your morning quote? Take a note of it and review what responses it elicited, Likes, Shares, and/or Comments.

While other people's research might be a guide, only you can know what your fans connect with. If you are unable to give the time to this research, then you should consider hiring a social media marketing company to look at your Page and spend some time gathering the data for you.

After The Like

You've hit a sweet spot and your number of fans has jumped from your 31 family and friends who know about your business to over 150 because of a recent radio interview. So what do you do now? How do you keep them engaged with your page and turn them into true fans who will share your messages and become the best promoters of your products?

You need a plan.

Why did you create the page? If your answer is because you heard somewhere that every business should be on Facebook then that won't help you reap any results from being there.

You need to intentionally plan what you will do on any social media. What do you want to say? Why do you want to say it that way? What is the desired response when people read or see what you've shared?

While you cannot predict what someone else will do with what you share online, you can increase the likelihood that they will interact with it in a way that benefits your business if you understand clearly what you are after.

Unless your business exists totally on Facebook or another social media then your plan must include a way for them to engage with you in the real world.

Do they sign up for your weekly newsletter of inspiration and marketing tips, do they click over to iTunes to buy your new single? Tell them what you want them to do with the information you've given them.

With so much information floating by on a daily basis, you cannot hope that enough people will see your posts. It will take a concerted effort for them to decide to click like and then go further and use what you've given.

If you store is having a sale then your online promotions should be focused on driving them in to your retail outlet. Use photos of new arrivals, offer discount coupons to fans who interact with a photo or status within a specific window of time.

Note that you never wait until you are about to have a sale to post on your page. Facebook actively promotes in your timeline the friends and pages you engage with frequently. If no one interacts with your page for weeks on end as you have not been posting, the chances of fans seeing your posts diminishes considerably.

Use Facebook to drive fans to your company website or to take another action. After they've liked your post they must be further encouraged to do something. This means what you share has to encourage re-sharing. Not because you've said "share this" but because the photo created an experience that others want to support or the status offers a solution or a thought that elicits a positive response.

DO

- Post often.
- Share inspiring photos.
- Keep your statuses short as it increases the chances they will be read.
- Respond to comments and messages in a timely fashion.
- Reshare interesting links from other people you admire.

DON'T

- Repost the same link 10 times in one day.
- Spam your friends' pages, groups and other fan pages.
- Focus only on your business.
- Forget to share links to your website.

4

Follow

When you visit a social media site that intrigues you, you can Subscribe to it or Follow it. From that point on you are notified via email each time the site is updated with new content. Several social media sites use the Follow concept, chief of which is Twitter. Pinterest and Instagram also use the Follow concept to encourage users to connect with other people on the platform. It is simply a different way of staying connected with what you are doing just as with Facebook.

We've already shared what the differences are among the platforms mentioned above, so how can you use Twitter for your business?

Twitter can be somewhat intimidating if you don't fancy yourself a wordsmith. How do you sound brilliant in 140 characters and is that enough time to engage a follower?

The key is not to see your activity on Twitter or any social media as a one-time interaction but as an ongoing conversation; a commitment you are making to stay connected and to share what is important to you.

For example, people will immediately question the motives of a politician who jumps on Twitter or Facebook four months before the election. Why? He is an unknown and he has not been engaging online with potential voters prior to the start of the election season. If all of his conversations take the tone of "Vote for Me" or "Mr. So and So Needs to be Voted Out", he is sending a very negative message about himself and will only attract the followers who enjoy trash talking in social spaces and are unlikely to show up to cast their ballot.

Newcomers to Twitter need a strategy that ensures that you don't sound as if you are merely there to gather votes but honestly want to engage followers to hear their views. Then you can present yourself as being able to implement the solutions.

The same is true for musicians, filmmakers, and authors who only remember their followers when they have something to sell. Twitter and other platforms are an opportunity to connect to people who are interested in your daily life. What are you passionate about besides yourself and your new book? What is your opinion on global issues? Who are the musicians who inspire you? What funny anecdote can you share about this morning's interaction with your child or a friend?

You must be ready to be vulnerable and open in the hopes that others will connect with you and want to support you and your initiatives whether they are political or artistic.

Remember to share what you have to offer or sell. However, overdo it and you can be quickly unfollowed.

The #Hashtag

It began as a way to categorize tweets but now the hashtag aka the pound (#) symbol has made its way unto other platforms. This symbol allows social media users to locate similar posts, find people with similar interests and generate conversation around a topic.

On Instagram, photos are filed around hashtags and so if you are posting images of Caribbean food, using #islandfood or #caribbeancuisine could get your images more traction as people search for images using these tags.

Hashtags are used to define what is trending. If you are sharing quotes on business or ICT or the Caribbean, including a hashtag in front of the word allows it to be found by other people globally using the same tags. This increases your exposure.

> **Special Note**: Facebook now uses the hashtag but it is often overused. A common misuse is to have a hashtag followed by an entire sentence with the spaces removed, for example, #iwenttothestore. The likelihood that other people are hashtagging the same long sentence is very small and so it defeats the purpose of using the hashtag.

Recently, global campaigns have been mobilized around a hashtag, which can bring awareness to important issues and generate interaction and most importantly drive change.

Do a search to find out what the popular hashtags are in your area of interest and if they differ on the various platforms you use. Begin to incorporate them into your social conversations.

DO

- Do respond to people who send you a direct message or have mentioned you in a tweet.
- Do retweet other people that you follow. Not just when they are tweeting about you but when they say something funny or meaningful that you agree with.
- Do retweet an earlier tweet if you believe it is worth repeating.

DON'T

- Don't spend all of your time filling your followers' timelines with retweets from others. They want to hear from you so say something.
- Don't disappear for weeks on end. Get help if you cannot post or tweet daily.
- Don't spend every 140 characters sharing a link to your business. Share photos and tips that your followers can use.

5

Lead

We've spoken of millions of people using the social spaces to build their businesses, including companies with significant funds available to promote their business. How do you compete? With all that virtual noise how do you stand out in the crowd?

The short answer is **Be Honest and Be Intentional**.

While some people get by on random posts on a multitude of platforms, if you really want to succeed you must have a strategy that you can measure in order to ascertain if the time and money you are spending on social media is benefiting your business.

Going back to our early conversation on setting SMART targets, it would be helpful to set out these targets in a worksheet. Define what activities you will do and on which platform over what period of time.

For example:

Facebook

❖ Share an inspiring photo or video

❖ Search for professionals, media sites and groups which are in your industry

❖ Join in and comment on the trending topic of the day

Twitter

❖ Search relevant industry hashtags

❖ Retweet two notable articles

❖ Find two interesting people to follow

❖ Comment back on tweets which mention your handle or on a hot topic on your timeline

Do this for each social platform you are on.

Social Media Editorial Calendar Template

DAY	7-9am	9-11am	11-1pm	1-3pm	3-5pm	5-7pm
FACEBOOK						
MON	Morning Inspiration		Weekend recap		3rd Party Post	
TUES		Blog Post				Promote Event
WED	Funny Post		Giveaway			Repost Blog
THUR	Throwback Thursday - Photo		Comment on the posts of other Fan Pages			Respond to fan comments on your posts
FRI	Fan of the Week					
SAT	Morning Funny					3rd Party Post
SUN						Inspiration
TWITTER						
MON	Morning Inspiration	Blog Post	RT 2 People			Respond to DMs
TUES	Quote of the Day		RT 2 People			Tweet to People
WED	3rd Party Post		RT 2 People			Join a Live Event
THUR	Share Infographic	Blog Post				
FRI	Follow Friday					
LINKEDIN						
MON	Blog Post					Join Group Discussion
TUES	3rd Party Post		Introduce yourself via Inbox. Personalize your message.			
WED	Congratulate Colleagues		Share Video			
THUR	Blog post		Endorse Contacts		Comment on posts relevant to your industry.	
FRI	Share Event Photo					

**RT= Retweet | DM = Direct Message

As you should be building your image as an expert in your field it is important that you share content you've created that reflects this.

Design an editorial calendar to help you stay on top of your social media strategy. The calendar should include your content list dealing with a variety of information relevant to your business such as history, company news, what's hot and your value proposition.

For example:

❖ Use the #tbt or #ThrowbackThursday to share a photo of your business from years past with a caption that reflects your consistency and adaptability. (Facebook, Instagram)
❖ Share a whitepaper or presentation on your primary industry specialty on LinkedIn and Twitter. Identify relevant keywords for hashtags.
❖ Identify what images, videos, blog posts will be used and on what platforms. What text will accompany the image? What time of day will they be shared?

Pay attention to trends and capitalize on online events which you can use to present yourself as having valuable knowledge to share.

Early in 2014 when winter storms continuously plagued the United States, many Caribbean tourism boards choose to share images of a snowman with his suitcase packed ready to head to warmer climates. It immediately sent the message that it is much warmer in the Caribbean and the unspoken suggestion that this time next year consider exchanging snow for sand.

If pictures used to tell 1000 words prior to social media, then today the right image shared at the perfect time can be worth more than a million words and money in the bank for you.

A flower from your garden can be the background of an inspiring quote. Be sure to include your twitter handle or web address on it so people can get to know more about the person behind the image. You can use Paint in Windows to add text or find one of hundreds of sites online which allow you to add text to your photos.

If you manage a blog, then ensure that your articles are not too long. Stick to 300 to 500 words and present useful information. If you must create a longer post, break it up into sections so that it does not feel overwhelming. Use Infographics, images and videos to support the article.

A blog post can be a photo and a question. You don't need to write a masterpiece every day. Consider that your job is to provide readers with a morning jolt of inspiration related to your core business. Do this in small manageable doses for more consistent and effective results.

Managing Your Social Media Presence

You don't need to be on every platform you've heard about. Start with one and master it before adding other social media accounts. As many of us don't have the luxury of time to respond to every tweet that we get in the time we get it, deploying platforms such as TweetDeck or HootSuite can be helpful. You are able to consolidate multiple social media accounts into one space and manage all of these interactions at a time that is convenient to you.

These platforms help you to plan your interactions. You can enter your status updates, photos, etc. in advance and set dates and times when they will go live. In that way, if you only have 30 minutes a day to dedicate to updating your pages you can have posts being shared at intervals while you are working elsewhere.

Branding

While getting into branding in all of its forms is beyond the scope of this book, it is important to know that branding includes the image and look, the words, service, and the experience that you offer.

Invest in a great design for your company logo, and the images used on your social spaces to promote your products and services. They need to be consistent across all of your platforms and they should also mirror what we would see if we were to visit your physical place of business.

Although you may only be active on one social platform you may wish to join others in the future. To build brand recognition be consistent with how you use your name on all platforms and the social handles/vanity link you select. Once you've decided on a name, sign up on the other social accounts to secure the names and to avoid social squatters.

Twitter only allows 15 characters – so if your brand name is longer than this abbreviate and use this abbreviation for the handle across all social media site. Use a tool like NameCheck to see if the one you want is available across all the popular social media sites.

If we were to go back to Jane and her boots, she could use the handle BootsByJane. Her social accounts should look like this:

❖ Twitter - @BootsByJane

❖ Facebook – www.facebook.com/BootsByJane

❖ Instagram - @BootsByJane

❖ Skype - @BootsByJane

Handling Detractors

Not everyone will be a true fan. Some people will enter your space for the sole purpose of pulling you down. While you could block them, it may be more useful to engage with them in a way that shows you do offer true value.

Be polite. Acknowledge their comment. Invite them to make a suggestion rather than simply put down what others have said. Find a way whenever possible to bring a resolution and when it is not possible, try to leave the conversation on a positive note.

You can gain new fans and customers by how you handle a negative comment.

Consistency is King

You created a fan page and you are still stuck at 59 likes. You tweet and no one retweets. You've read all of the guides on doing social media right and still you are not seeing any changes. Don't give up.

We've bought the fallacy that with more than a billion people on social media surely we can get a few thousand. However, even when we get those numbers they are not interacting and certainly not buying.

You've got to be patient. You've got to be consistent. People know when you are not genuine. People know when you are only interested in yourself and your business.

Be committed to using social media to spread the positives about your company and how you are serving the world. We gravitate to people and causes that are making a difference. Use your social spaces to show how you are doing that; whether by giving back to the community, celebrating the work of others, and offering solutions through the services or products you sell.

Remember your online world needs to support your offline activities. If they are not working in tandem, fans and followers will feel this disconnect. Use offline channels such as newspaper ads, press releases, radio commercials, events to increase your online traffic. Your social media content must give guidance as to what they should do next. Click to register, download a free gift, and visit your store to use the coupon, or donate to a cause.

The clearer you are about what you want people to do with your company, the easier it will be to convey this message through the social media spaces of your choosing.

DIY Social Media vs Outsourcing

While I manage social media accounts for clients, I'm a proponent for DIY social media and here's why. One, if your funds are limited it can be costly to have someone manage your accounts effectively in order to see results. You won't see the results you want overnight. Two, your voice will be authentic. This is not to say you use bad grammar and don't spell check before posting but you can have a burst of inspiration, see an image that immediately captures what is beautiful about your product, your location or business that when you share it, people will connect with. To put it through the filter of a social media expert means you lose the moment and the emotion. The best way to deal with the latter is that both you and your consultant have access to the accounts so you can share as well when the need arises.

If you are really pressed for time and have the resources to hire someone as part of your marketing strategy then find a consultant who understands marketing in all of its forms. You don't need someone who says they specialize in social media but don't understand traditional marketing. They will need to be able to move between the various worlds for you to have the greatest impact and to generate revenue.

Pay Attention

Social media continues to adapt and transform and as such you will need to give some time to reading up on changes and how they may affect your online presence. Subscribe to blogs that offer social media tips for small business so you can have a ready pool of ideas to try out.

Most of all, take the step and decide you will use these readily available tools to help your business to grow.

DO

- Create a worksheet to set out your goals and plans for working on social media.
- Do use a variety of content formats (video, photos, blogs, infographics).
- Do measure the effectiveness of each type of content.
- Use the same handle/vanity name on all social spaces.

DON'T

- Ignore trends. Find a way to connect your conversations to the discussions of others.
- Miss an opportunity to answer or bring resolution to a complaint from a customer if they do it online.
- Try to be on every social platform. Start with one and master it before adding others.

More to Learn

There is always more to learn as social media and the ways in which we use them evolve.

If you aren't on any social media platforms presently here is a list of the platforms and other websites mentioned in this book.

Amazon – www.amazon.com

Facebook - www.facebook.com

Goodreads – www.goodreads.com

Google Plus – https://plus.google.com

HootSuite – www.hootsuite.com

Instagram – www.instagram.com

LinkedIn – www.linkedin.com

NameCheck – www.namechk.com

Pinterest – www.pinterest.com

Skype – www.skype.com

Slideshare – www.slideshare.net

TweetDeck – www.tweetdeck.com

Twitter – www.twitter.com

YouTube – www.youtube.com

You can find other useful tips on growing your business with social media on my learning portal at www.trulycaribbean.net.

www.ingramcontent.com/pod-product-compliance
Lightning Source LLC
Chambersburg PA
CBHW051825170526
45167CB00005B/2164

9781500139902